I0158643

GROOMING GREATNESS

7 PRINCIPLES TO DISCOVER YOUR PURPOSE, CREATE MULTIPLE INCOME STREAMS, AND ENJOY ENDLESS PROFITS

MARQUES YOUNG

WWW.MARQUESYOUNGPUBLISHING.COM

TABLE OF CONTENTS

ACKNOWLEDGEMENT

This is by far the most difficult part of writing this book!

Many have been influential in my life. However, I dedicate this book to the following people. Your impact is invaluable and inspired me to publish this for the world to read and enjoy. I thank you dearly.

My Lovely Wife, Tanya Young
- Your unending love and support for Sydney and I is remarkable. Without you this is impossible.

My Phenomenal Daughter, Sydney Williams
- You inspire me to be more courageous every day.

My Parents, Michael & Otelia Young
- You raised me to become a great man with high moral character.

My Grandparents, The Late J.B. and Agnes Stewart
- No one will ever understand how much you mean to me. I think about you every day and cannot wait until we all meet again.

My Grandparents, Wilbert and Ella Young
- You taught me the value and importance of quiet and humble servitude. Silent leadership is rare.

My Bishop and Mentor, Dr. Todd M. Hall
- Your example and mentorship are the impetus for this book. I love and admire you more than words can express. May God keep you and continue to use you for His glory.

FORWARD

I never imagined that I would one day write a book and allow the world access to my personal thoughts and experiences. However, my life has been positively impacted so greatly within the past year through my newly rekindled relationship with God, a closer bond and connection with my wife and daughter, a transformation of my circle of friends and other relationships, and a new outlook on my future. These changes have allowed me to become more comfortable with being me and to tap into the greatness that is promised and ordained for me.

As a result, I was compelled to publicly offer some of my testimonies and experiences so that you can also make positive life changes and transformations to tap into your greatness and become an inspiration for others. So, welcome aboard, and I hope to give value in reading my very first book with a sense of perspective, inspiration, motivation, and faith to achieve a better relationship with God, to have personal and financial success, and to Groom The Greatness within you!

INTRODUCTION

This book is my very first book and publication to the masses. It is about my personal story and journey as a premature baby, who was only given 30 days to live, born into a rural, low-middle class family in Tennessee to become a College Graduate, Father, Husband, Loyal Friend, Established Engineer and Manager of the largest ice cream manufacturing facility in the world, Entrepreneur, Financial Coach, Motivational Speaker, Author and Publishing Company Owner.

As I have matured and unknowingly become an inspiration to others, it is evident to me that everyone has a story and a journey to share with others that will make a difference in the world. Regardless of your circumstances, you can overcome. You can be as successful and as happy as you desire by walking in your purpose. While doing so, you will create unlimited financial wins and have continuous residual income and profits as you share your journey and story with others. The only requirement is that you believe in yourself. Once you believe in you and your purpose, you will become rich and wealthy beyond your wildest dreams.

I am sick and tired of listening to and watching people focus on negative situations and circumstances and complain about why they cannot do or accomplish something. In this book you will learn how your story has similarities with mine. You will discover why I am sick and tired of people not taking advantage of opportunities, whether big or small, to take action to make a change in their lives for the better. I will tell you why you should stop focusing on what others think or say about you and start focusing on what you think you can do to become the very best person you can be.

You will see that you can tap into your greatness and attain anything you desire once you start walking in your purpose and making yourself happy first. Living and walking in your purpose is not being selfish. It is being self-starting, self-motivating and selfless in every aspect. This newfound approach to living your life will be so impactful to you and to others that you will find every moment of every day special and endless because you are permanently fulfilling your desires as you help others do the same.

Throughout this book I will touch on aspects such as self-worth, family, friends, employment, careers, personal finances, time and God. All of the aforementioned things are present in the daily grind called life for virtually everyone that I can imagine who walks the face of this earth. Some may be more or less important within your life, but I guarantee you that it has an impact. Your purpose and your impact will touch these same areas but in your special way. Whether you are young, old, rich, poor, male, female, short, tall, healthy, sick, weak or strong, you must identify your purpose and tap into your greatness and continue to groom your greatness to live a fulfilled and successful life.

Before I get into the details, let me be perfectly clear...you can run from your purpose, but you cannot hide. Your purpose will always follow you everywhere you go. You can deny it and hope to find some other thing to make you happy and successful, but you will never have both happiness and success until you identify, acknowledge, and walk in your purpose to become great. It is at this point that you will open every door for success – self-esteem, self-worth, family, friends, employment, career, personal finances and faith.

Life is extremely simple and straightforward. You will see how and why as I explain my purpose and share my story so you can tap into and groom your greatness and make profits doing so. Let's eliminate the complexity in this book so you can tap into and continue

to groom your greatness and never have a financial worry again!

CHAPTER 1: HAVE A DREAM...NOW CHASE IT!

"Don't worry about failures. Worry about the chances you miss when you don't even try." – Jack Canfield

Happiness, Greatness & Success Isn't As Hard As We Believe

One of the biggest things that I've learned over the past year is that we as humans have many basic needs - water, food, shelter and love. No matter where you go, who you meet, or who you know, each and every person has these same basic needs and desires. Unfortunately, once these basic needs are met, society then dictates our thoughts and understanding as to who should be allowed or given more than these basic needs and be happy with their lives. Yes, happiness is a need that we all have, but the extent of happiness varies and is dependent upon each individual to determine what makes them happy. Simultaneously, one's happiness centers on how successful they are in comparison to others in life. Whether it is school, work, sports, games, politics, etc., everyone is compared to one another, and this comparison lends to competition. Everyone is competing for something in life - better grades, better jobs, better homes, better cars, more money, more opportunities, etc.

I can go on and on about the search of happiness, comparison, and competition forever, but I am choosing not to do so. Instead, I am stopping just as I stopped comparing myself to others and ruining my happiness trying to be or mimic what was deemed as successful or great in the public eye. The key learning for me in 2013 was to be happy with me because no one else could be happy for me as much as I can be. No one else can judge or critique my happiness more critically than me. So, why would I continue the failed attempts to chase society's view of success, greatness and happiness if it was not previously satisfying my needs?

The moment I changed my perspective and my attitude towards success was the exact moment I became happy and tapped into my greatness. God allowed me to move my emotions and feelings aside and focus on me. Public opinion no longer ruled my personal perspective, and suddenly, I was able to see my purpose, my path, and my assignment in life. With this book, I am starting to fulfill my purpose and my assignment...provide a platform, be an inspiration for others, and help you groom your greatness!

The reason I say happiness, greatness and success isn't as hard as we believe is because only you control your happiness and create your own vision and definition of greatness and success. In order to achieve greatness and success, you must follow these principles:

1. **Change your attitude about things.** Be positive and focus on your opportunities instead of focusing on your challenges. Do not allow negativity to permeate and dominate your thoughts and your attitude towards situations, circumstances and events. Maintaining a positive mindset is critical to overcoming challenges and negative situations.

2. **Dare to be different.** It's okay to be different, because no one else can or will be you. You want different things and results in life from everyone else. Some may be the same, but none are the exactly the same as the next person. So, stop comparing yourself to others and compare yourself to you. Strive to be better today than you were yesterday. If you improve each and every day, you will become successful and achieve greatness.

3. **Encourage yourself and others to execute and live by the first two principles.** Immediately, you will begin to see your circles change and see your positivity become

contagious. All of these new experiences will develop into new opportunities and being different will stick. As you develop these new relationships and take advantage of your opportunities, you will breakthrough the doubt and glass ceilings you and others have placed before you and do great things.

As you make this personal transformation, know that everyone is watching. Most people generally watch in silence or from afar, but they are definitely watching. So, you may was well give them something good to watch!

As you make this personal transformation, know that everyone is talking. Most people generally talk in silence or from afar, but they are definitely talking. So, you may was well give them something good to talk about!

As you make this personal transformation, know that everyone is waiting, waiting on you to revert back to the old you because they are accustomed to the old you and not ready for you to change as much as you want to change. So, you may as well change your situation and ask them why they are waiting to change! While standing still, even a man with no legs can pass you by if he is making an effort to change his position despite his visible challenges and physical differences.

Start your journey to be great today, right now! Start chasing your dreams. Push yourself to step outside of the box, step outside of your comfort zone once per day and see what happens. You will be surprised at what progress will be made and how easy it is to tap into the greatness within you!

CHAPTER 2: PLAN YOUR WORK & WORK YOUR PLAN

"Hope is neither a viable option nor a sustainable plan." – Marques Young

The Power of Planning & Persistence

When I was seven years old, one day my dad asked me did I want to play organized baseball. Being the energetic kid that I was, I said, "YES"! Never mind the fact I had never played baseball before at any point in my life. I went into it headlong and was so excited on my first day of practice. I was out there with new kids that I didn't know…other 6-7 year olds, some of which had played baseball before unlike myself. My excitement quickly turned into embarrassment.

Some things you never forget in life no matter how long ago it happened. We were in centerfield going through pop up drills. Coaches would gather a small group of us and take us out to centerfield with a bucket of balls. They lined us up single file and tossed the ball in the air about ten feet to simulate a pop up being hit from the bat for us to catch. Remember when I said that I had never played baseball before now. Well, it was my turn in line to go next. As I approached the spot to stand and look at the coach, he was staring at me rather wildly and did not toss the ball in the air. He walked up to me and said, "Son, you have your glove on the wrong hand. You don't even know how to put a glove on."

I'm sure he did not mean to embarrass me, but he did. It wasn't his constructive feedback that hurt me as he was helping me put my glove on the right hand. It was the laughter of my teammates that stung the most. I learned in that moment at an early age that people will laugh at you while you are struggling. People will see you not doing the right thing and not help you. Needless to say, I struggled in my first year playing baseball. The only reason I got off the bench to play in games was due to the league fairness rules that required coaches to have every player in the game for at least one inning. I would always get put into the game in the last inning and rarely had a chance to bat due to my late game insertion into the lineup. I believe I had less than 10 at-bats during my 10 or so games during the season with maybe one hit.

During the offseason and time period before the next baseball season, my dad played some catch with me, and I would go outside to play catch with myself. Yes, I played catch with myself. I got creative. I would toss a tennis ball off the roof of the house and pretend that I was catching popups and line drives from hitters. We had concrete steps leading to our front door with a small walk way about seven feet long that led to the sidewalk and street. These steps were the steps to my greatness as a baseball player moving forward. They allowed me to practice all types of fielding and increase my hand-eye coordination and agility by throwing a tennis ball into the steps. Everything from ground balls, popups, line drives and bloop hits were simulated daily for hours on end. I went from that kid that no one wanted to see in the game because I didn't know how to put my glove on properly to an All-Star the very next season.

Every year thereafter I made the All-Star team. For the next eight years, I was one of the elite players in the area making the All-Star team and playing every position, including pitcher and catcher. I eventually played high school baseball and was on a few traveling teams. There was one baseball accomplishment that I had a difficult time reaching – hitting a homerun. I never really thought about hitting home runs because my skill set was a reliable contact hitter who could get on base and disrupt the pitcher with my speed and ability as a great base runner.

After playing for nearly eight years, all of my friends had hit a home run at some point in their life. Even some kids who had never made an All-Star team. They had gotten lucky to achieve greatness as a hitter in their eyes. Frustrated with myself, one day I made my mind up that I was going to hit a home run. The day I decided was not conducive for me to do so for a few reasons.

Remember, my parents believed in education and I loved being challenged academically as well. Prior to my junior year of high school, I attended an academic summer camp at Tennessee Technological University (TTU) in Cookeville, TN, to study engineering. Yes, I was the literal little nerd! I made a decision to miss some of my summer baseball season, which was a difficult one because of my dream of playing college baseball one day and needing to get as much practice time and games under my belt to get better, to attend this four-week intensive pre-engineering program. After completing the program, which propelled me into my current career as an engineer, I immediately returned home and had a game the very next day.

During those four weeks at TTU, I didn't as much as see a baseball much less practice. My traveling team was full of great players from the area. They had played nearly eight games that week and needed to rest some guys. With no practice or prep time, I was inserted into the starting lineup batting third as if I had not missed the last four weeks. A little nervous, I believe I grounded out in my first at-bat and struck out the next at-bat. However, we were hitting the ball well as a team that night and had a lead going into the latter innings.

Just prior to my third at-bat, I looked at three or four of my teammates in the dugout, and I vividly remember telling them "I'm hitting a homerun my next at-bat". Immediately they all laughed saying that I couldn't because I had never hit a homerun and wouldn't based on my time away and previous poor at-bats that night.

I shrugged off the laughs. I kept telling myself I would do it. I visualized myself hitting a homerun over the left-field fence. This inner motivation continued from the dugout to the on-deck circle and then into the batter's box as I approached the plate for my third at-bat. I dug one foot inside the batter's box and held one hand up to the umpire indicating time out until I gathered myself for the first pitch. The entire time I'm telling myself, "Marques you're going to hit a homerun over the leftfield fence on the very first pitch." As the pitcher placed his feet on the rubber and wound up, I saw the ball before it left his hand. I saw the seams on the ball midway to the plate. I swung and saw the ball fly off the bat into left field. I bolted out of the batter's box heading for first base. Knowing I made good contact, I thought to myself 'I have a double for sure'. As I neared first base, I looked up for the ball and saw it clear the left field wall.

In all of my years of seeing others hit homeruns and watching the Major Leaguers hit them as well, everyone would slowly and gracefully take their home run trot around the bases. I always envisioned myself doing the same whenever I hit my first homerun, but it didn't quite happen that way for me. I sprinted around the bases as if a rabid dog was chasing me. Rounding third with lightning speed, I darted towards home plate and touched it with both feet and stood there tall for a brief second and darted back into the dugout.

All of my teammates were happily cheering for me. Although I was happy, I was also disgusted. Why was I disgusted in one of the happiest moments of my baseball career? I was disgusted because my teammates did not believe in me. The very individuals who knew how reliable and consistent I was did not believe in me or in my dream and ability to hit a homerun.

Immediately upon entering the dugout, I fell into my purpose at that moment but did not know it at the time. I spent the next couple of minutes giving an impromptu inspirational rant to my entire team explaining how I motivated myself and believed in myself despite you not believing in me. My self-motivation gave me the result that I wanted and desired, and neither you nor anyone else will ever deny me again.

As the summer ended and we closed out the season, I hit another homerun with this one going even farther, and nearly hit three more within a five game span. The power of the mind and visualizing success is a powerful thing. I had accomplished what seemed to be the impossible for me over the past eight years on more than one occasion within a few weeks time, and soon my teammates began to expect homeruns and even greater things of me as a hitter and a leader after that night at the ballpark.

The moral of my story is simple. Expect greatness and you will soon achieve it!

CHAPTER 3: TAKE IMMEDIATE ACTION

"If you really want to do something, you will find a way. If you don't, you'll find an excuse." – Jim Rohn

Dreams Versus Goals

We often hear people talk about having dreams...these could be dreams one has in their sleep, day dreams to escape the chaos or stress of the moment, or dreams of aspirations to do or accomplish new things in life. Dreams are great because they allow our minds to wander into a space of creativity and infinite possibilities to imagine a state of happiness, bliss and abundance.

You may be asking yourself "what is the big deal"? What is the difference between dreams and goals? Fortunately for us, there is a significant difference between the two that allows us to make our dreams a reality. Therein lies the beauty of goals. Goals are specific visualizations of the dream where we place specific, time-bound parameters on ourselves or on our situations to make the said dream(s) become reality. The critical path in making these dreams a goal and these goals a reality is ACTION.

I've experienced many sleep dreams that have come to pass in some form or fashion in my conscious state. We typically refer to these types of occurrences as deja vu. I believe these instances are God's way of validating the prophetic voice and vision in each of us. It is then our responsibility to maintain our faith in Him to make these dreams, seemingly coincidental visions derived in our sleep and semi-conscious states, a reality. However, many times we fail to take this gift and put ACTION towards it to transform this dream into a goal, and ultimately, into an accomplishment with tangible results through faith in His word and His ordained promise for our lives.

ACTION is required. It is not an option. Failure to take action leaves these dreams as merely dreams. Dreams generally deferred due to mental blocks or a lack of faith that the "impossible" can become possible. Always look at the word impossible differently as I'M POSSIBLE!

ACTION is also required because we must put in hard work and consistent effort to reap the rewards of our toils and labor. I don't recall any successful harvest of crops without farmers working long, hard hours over the course of an entire season until the crop is ready for harvesting. Once the harvest season is reached, the farmer

21

then works even harder to complete the harvest before the crop is ruined due to weather and soil changes that are meant for a different crop in a different season. A lack of action leads to wasted resources, wasted opportunities, wasted time, and wasted future harvests. Always act immediately with the intention of making forward progress.

Take advantage of the dreams that you are given as gifts for you to develop goals to become great, to become successful, to change your life for the better in every season. No matter how outlandish or how impossible of a dream you think you may have, it can become your reality with effective goal setting and ACTION on your behalf to make that dream come true for you.

Set high expectations for yourself with specific, time-bound goals. Ask God for what you want. Believe that you will accomplish your goals. Claim that the end result will be yours. You must ACT to deliver ACTION (the accomplishment of a thing usually over a period of time, in stages, or with the possibility of repetition) on your goals.

Keep dreaming big dreams. Keep dreaming many dreams. Never give up on your dreams. Set high expectations and goals. Now comes the important part...**Ready...Set...ACTION!**

CHAPTER 4: TIME IS OF THE ESSENCE...USE YOUR TIME WISELY

"Time is what we want most but what we use worst." – William Penn

The Composition of Time

Time for the vast majority of us is simple. It is the basic literal definition as prescribed in Webster's Dictionary - the thing that is measured as seconds, minutes, hours, days, years, etc. Webster's also defines time as:

- the measured or measurable period during which an action, process or condition exists or continues

- a nonspatial continuum that is measured in terms of events which succeed one another from past through present to future

- the point or period when something occurs

- an appointed, fixed or customary moment or hour for something to happen, begin or end

- an opportune or suitable moment - often used in the phrase "about time"

- And there are many other definitions for time...

These literal definitions of time and many other things within our lives require a much deeper analysis in order to maximize our individual potential that God has given and promised to each of us. Time is more than the basic definition. Time is more than the additional documented definitions that man has prescribed.

As I embark on this topic of TIME, I fully know that there will be something that resonates with you, and maybe more than one, to transform your life and start your new journey to greatness. What I've grown to learn and believe is that each individual already has the ability to be great and successful. However, the great divide between those who become great and those who remain average, mediocre or even below average is the person's ability to take advantage of their TIME. So, you may ask yourself "what do you mean by taking advantage of your time"? Allow me to explain.

Let's revisit what time is. Yes, both Webster's Dictionary and society often and overwhelming refer to time in its literal definition...seconds, minutes, hours, days, years, etc.; the point or period when something occurs; the measured or measurable period during which an action, process or condition exists or continues. Time is also that moment when something happens. All of these are

26

indeed correct, tried, true, and verified. However, what these definitions do not tell you directly is that time is dependent upon how you view, treat, utilize, share and value it.

Let me make sure you did not miss what I just said and how powerful that last statement is and will be in your future. Science and math cannot be denied. A second is a second. A minute is a minute. An hour is an hour. A year is a year. You cannot and will not change how these are measured on a finite level. The fundamental difference in these measured moments is the composition of that moment.

What is meant by the composition of a moment? Think about a picture or a photograph. The saying "a picture is worth a thousand words" means that you can convey so much in a picture more easily and readily than you can with words. Pictures are universal and tell a story better and more dynamically than words on a page. Pictures leave strong mental images that last a lifetime. A moment's composition is just the same. Within the same time frame, and let us use one minute as an example, you can either completely waste, partially waste, or maximize the full potential of that one minute. The level to which you utilize and value that minute in time will change your composition of that moment in time.

Most team sports are played within a time frame that dictates the start of the game and end of the game. During this specified time frame, the teams, players, and coaches employ strategies, scripted plays, and substitutions to take advantage of game situations that are heavily predicated upon the time remaining in the game. In critical situations, especially when the score is close and time is running out in the final moments of the game, timeouts are typically used to gather the team together to discuss the situation, devise a plan or play, and return to the game to run a specific play to score or prevent the other team from scoring to win the game. These timeouts and team huddles are taken and executed to ensure everyone knows the plan and strategy in order to maximize the time to reach the goal...to win the game.

It is this composition within the final moments that makes the critical difference between organization and chaos, winning and losing, failure and success, average and greatness. In this particular example, many things could have transpired in the game between the players on the team. However, utilizing the timeout to refocus, develop awareness, and gain alignment, allows the players to function as a unit and put themselves in a situation to be successful.

Understand that success could happen without the timeout and it's ability to compose the moment, but success and greatness is more probable when the time is used wisely with a clear goal, alignment of strategy, and definitive purpose.

You must view your life in the same lens as sports teams do in these critical situations. Your life is critical because you only have one life to live. Don't believe the YOLO (You Only Live Once) hype. In case you haven't noticed, those who publicly follow the YOLO principle may not be the best role models to emulate! Yes, we do only live once, but you should not throw caution to the wind living frivolously and waste your time. There are no timeouts in life. You cannot put life on pause. The world and everyone in it will continue to move on if you do "take a timeout".

Understand that you can take a timeout, but make sure you do so with the desire and intent to positively change your situation. Compose that moment to say the TIME is OUT for what I was doing, how I was responding, how I was behaving, how I was living. Make the very next moment leaving the TIME-OUT your new future.

Use your time wisely. Treat it with tender loving care. Do not allow anyone to waste your time, devalue your time, or monopolize your time. Do not allow yourself to do the same either.

You must view time as the most valuable thing you have and own in

this world. How you use this time will develop the composition of

your moments and your life. Time lost cannot be regained. You have

the capability, ability and authority to determine if you compose

nothing or compose a masterpiece. It is your TIME to decide.

A Matter of Life & Death

The previous section centered on the composition of time and

how one utilizes their time to create special moments in time. These

moments ultimately create your pathway to greatness and success. I

recently endured the loss of a loved one, my Grandmother. Although

she departed from us physically, her spirit and her legacy live on both

through myself and everyone else that she encountered in life. The

reason why is not because she's my Grandmother, and it's the right or

good thing to say. It is because she fulfilled her assignment. Two

things are guaranteed to happen to each of us –- (1) Life and (2)

Death -- and between these two column-posts lies time. What you

make of that time is your legacy, and your legacy will always live on

through time.

Once the music stops, the crowds stop cheering, that last lap is run around the race track, you say your last words, make your last impressions, and you take your last breath, the world keeps on going. All that remains of you are memories. Those memories are then deeply reflected upon by others. Those reflections are critical images of time that are each and every composition of the moments that people shared with you. The path of life and death are lived simultaneously in the minds, thoughts and emotions of others in those reflective moments of time.

Thus, your time is a figurative matter of life and death. Your life and your death will be compared to your time shared and spent, maximized and wasted, loved and disliked, wanted and unwanted. Regardless, your life will be reviewed over and over for the rest of eternity. Your legacy is now all that remains.

Alternately, your time is a literal matter of life and death. Your life and your death already have the time stamps identified by God. There is only one question this time regarding time. That question is "How are you going to make your time count with God"?

We've often heard the phrase "being in the wrong place at the wrong time". I don't really believe in this saying because we all make decisions, we all have choices. You choose to go against what God has told you to do. That little voice in your head (often referred to as our conscience) in certain moments is God's way of directing you to do what is intended for you to do at that point in time. We either choose to listen and obey or to disregard Him and disobey. What happens next determines your future.

You determine whether or not you fulfill your assignment. Before you can fulfill the assignment, you must learn and understand your assignment. This realization only occurs once you take the time to develop a relationship with God, spend time with God, and put in the effort to walk in your purpose. I admire many things about my Grandmother. One of the most important things that I admire is her dedication to her purpose in life. She poured everything she had into her purpose and her assignment. It was only recently, merely days before she moved on to be with the Lord, that I truly understood and appreciated how she fulfilled her assignment. As I wrote these last few words and prepared to celebrate her life on the day of her funeral, I was so happy and joyful. No, I never imagined that I would feel this way about losing a loved one and someone so close to me. Yet, I smile. I smile because her time, her purpose, and her assignment allowed me to reach this point in my life. Her assignment has allowed me to walk in my purpose.

My purpose is to speak life into you. My purpose is to do many other things that I have yet to learn and understand, but as I walk in my purpose, my assignment will be fulfilled, and my time will be maximized so that I will live in my death and never fail my Father's intent for my life. Do not live and not leave a legacy of fulfillment. Use your time so that your life and your death will be great times for others to share your story, your legacy, your purpose and your assignment so that they can inspire others to do the same.

Trust Your Time & Your Timing

When I started this piece on time, I had a palpable sense of urgency to express both my personal experiences and my conversations with God to my audience. As I continued to write this piece on time, I was given a new subject to discuss, but before making the transition, I have one final piece to illustrate regarding time. This last piece in the TIME discussion, at least for the time being, centers on the ideal of trust. You must trust that you will have faith in your works and in God's word that you are operating within your time and season to fulfill your assignment and purpose.

What I love so much about God and His infinite wisdom is that He never fails to come right on time. The transition that I'm making as we depart from time is not a tangential subject but a specific and direct bridge to the next topic of intuition. I'm following my intuition based on my conversations and interactions with God to help those reading this book to do just the same. Now is not the time to have doubt and worry about what others will say or do in response to your actions. Now is the time to be bold, forthright, specific, deliberate, direct and helpful in everything that you do.

In case you haven't noticed, we are exposed to just the opposite of what is needed right now. Each and every day in the news, on our jobs, in our homes, with our loved ones and friends, we skirt around the heart of subjects and matters of the day because it is easy, convenient, comfortable and non-confrontational with those of different beliefs and perspectives. For example, Malaysian Airlines Flight 370 cannot be a great mystery to those in high places within the Malaysian government and other well-to-do and powerful spheres of the world. 9-11 was not a mystery to these same types of individuals. The recent economic downturn in the United States did not happen by some fluke arrangement of events and circumstances. The Ebola virus outbreak and scares around the world and the United States were not surprises. People who could prevent such things from occurring or provide ample notice of these events chose not to for various reasons. Meanwhile, everyone on the outside looking in wondered in amazement at how such a drastic set of events could take place.

We all must come to the realization and understanding in these times that the time is out to turn a blind eye. We typically either completely fail to pay attention or only pay attention to what is comfortable, positive, and easy to explain. We must be very attentive to what is going on around us just as closely as we watch clocks. Every clock, watch or device made to tell time is slightly different in the accuracy of the time. However, you can and will provide definitive answers to questions and fulfill your purpose if the intricate mechanism of your chronometer is dialed in and operating at peak performance.

The same holds true with taking control of how you utilize your time and step into your purpose. You already possess the mechanisms and items necessary to determine if you are on track and on time. Oftentimes, the missing link is your inner faith to trust yourself enough to walk in your purpose once it is identified and defined. Had individuals taken the responsibility to inform the public about the aforementioned disasters (e.g., Flight 370, 9-11, Economic downturn, etc.), the likelihood of these events taking place and being such historical events of tragedy and despair would be slim to none.

Only you know when it is your time, what you should do with your time, and how to use your time to make a difference. I've already told you that time does not stop. You cannot reverse it, and you cannot relive it. However, you can easily waste it and allow other things and people to monopolize it. Just this week as I wrote this text I allowed some things to transpire in my life that could have nearly killed me had I not taken the time to address them. Exactly what I previously discussed regarding time being a matter of life and death is real.

Trust your intuition. Keep your eyes on your chronometer so that you know where you are at all times so that you can respond in time. Be bold, forthright, specific, deliberate, direct and helpful in your actions at all times. You never know when you will fulfill a portion of your assignment because there is always a time when you can and will be on time for someone in their time of need.

CHAPTER 5: MAINTAIN YOUR FAITH & FOLLOW YOUR INTUITION

"The will of a man is his greatest test. Press on, push through and be great." – Marques Young

Faith, Intuition & Your Future

After sharing my thoughts and experiences with others, I soon understood my purpose in life through a series of fortunate events that transpired primarily due to my renewed positive attitude and the Laws of Attraction. As we embark on this next series, you must follow your instincts and intuition as have I with this book and this new approach to my life to have a bigger, better and brighter future so that you can do the same.

For those who do not know me, I consider myself to be scholarly and eager to share knowledge with others. Therefore, let's define intuition. According to Webster's Dictionary:

> *Intuition -- a natural ability or power that makes it possible to know something without any proof or evidence: a feeling that guides a person to act a certain way without fully*

understanding why; something that is known or understood

without proof or evidence.

It is this very definition of intuition that is the core of every decision and choice that we as individuals make in life. God has provided each of us with a strong sense of intuition meant to be the great equalizer in all situations. I say it is an equalizer because every one is different and every situation is different. Your desires and expectations are likely different than the next person, yet we tend to go with majority decisions, thoughts or wishes because we do not want to "disrupt the apple cart" or "go against the grain or status-quo" for many different reasons. It could be because it is easy, less controversial, expected, or the within that ever-dreaded comfort zone. Your intuition is important because your inner being and connection to and with God is centered around your intuition which is generally sub-conscious thought designed to be manifested into real actions and words for the world to see so that you can attain what is specifically destined for you.

The previous points can be discussed in great detail and have been by many scholars, philosophers, clergy, and great minds of the world for centuries. My aim is not to make any attempts to either redistribute previous thoughts or dissertations but to force you to begin to think...think about how you are living your life with respect to your intuition. Are you following your intuition 100% of the time and maximizing your potential and destiny? Are you following your intuition less than 100% of the time and partially living your potential and destiny? Are you never following your intuition and struggling to find answers as to why negative or undesirable things happen in your life?

Timing is critical to the concept and use of intuition as well. We've previously spoken about time and it's importance. Time and intuition are closely coupled like intricately designed gears on a complex mechanical system to deliver efficient and effective motion and results with minimal force and effort. Misuse or ineffective use of your time and your intuition will definitely yield undesired and poor results. Do not doubt your instinctive thoughts, feelings and critical awareness from God. These sub-conscious and seemingly psychic or prophetic visions are intended for your use in life to take the necessary steps towards your greatness and the fulfillment of your purpose.

It is amazing how God has instilled this strong and innate ability in each of us to view the future without full understanding. Spend less time attempting to rationalize events and situations and more time acting on this great gift that has been imparted upon you. God is definitely working as I follow my intuition and walk in my purpose. Just today I was humbled to learn how this section of the book has impacted the life of a family that I do not know. The family is committing their one-year-old son to Christ today and shared the following with me:

1. The father/husband is fighting through his 2nd bought of brain cancer...a fight that I have learned is being won with great success.

2. The father/husband has renewed his faith in God.

3. The father/husband has taken action to improve his family's future despite his cancer.

4. The Father is guiding the father/husband to deliver the family into greatness!

5. Four months after writing this the father/husband is now 100% cancer free and has moved his family into a larger

home, has more income, and lives a much more stress free
and happy life!

GOD IS GOOD!!!

Walking in your greatness will yield immeasurable results and
benefits for yourself and others. God's grace, mercy and glory will
deliver people from disease, despair, poverty, physical illness, mental
illness, jealously, addiction, depression, and any other transgressions
and struggles occurring in life. Your walk must be addressed with full
faith in God and the intuition He has provided for you. William
Wordsworth once said "faith is passionate intuition", and I truly
believe this statement.

Trusting Your Instincts

As I wrote this book, it took me a while to write this chapter
for many reasons, but primarily because I took some time to focus on
some things. There was no real downtime during this hiatus, yet I
was able to manage to use the little downtime that I did have to think
and re-think about what is important to me. After doing so, I was
able to re-focus and provide more of my thoughts and give value.

Everything we do in life centers around trust and instincts. For example, we generally trust ourselves enough to drive to jobs or to our homes without thinking about the route to take because it's so familiar. While driving, you do not even think about where you're going or the route you take to get there. Your instincts unconsciously get you to your destination because it's such a routine. You unconsciously trust your instincts.

During the weeks that it took me to compose this chapter, I learned to trust myself and, more importantly, to trust my instincts in order to maximize my life and be great. I made the conscious decision to follow my instincts and not over analyze or second-guess myself. You will think of this book and everything associated with me as a center and circle of trust because my intuition is that you are looking for it just like I have been within myself.

By no means am I saying that I'm perfect or a guru on anything. What I will say and guarantee you is everything you get from me is 100% real, authentic, and genuine. I'm completely walking in my purpose now and putting in the work to fulfill my assignment. I am an expert on my journey and my life. God has given me a great gift and an amazing assignment that I cherish. One thing I can give my expert opinion on is you can get anything you want out of life by living and walking in your purpose per God's plan for you.

It took me over one month to write this particular chapter. That month was a complete whirlwind with virtually no time to think. However, I had enough time to think because I made the time to think and put some action into those thoughts. I realized that my greatness was and has always been within me. I was just too stubborn to get out of my own way so I can be great. Once I removed that roadblock, I was able to do so much in a very short amount of time with relative ease. Besides traveling over 3,000 miles in that month, I became a better husband, father, listener (contrary to my wife's opinion at times), mentor and leader. I also became more aware of my personal needs that were always placed on the back burner.

Yes, chosen people who walk in their purpose and fulfill their assignments oftentimes neglect themselves which causes them to derail their ability to meet their standard of greatness. That is why I was so grateful for that month. I was more selfish which allowed me to become more aware of my instincts and more attuned with fulfilling my assignment and being great.

God has provided you with intuition and instincts just like animals that live and thrive on instinct. Trust and follow your instincts. You will find that the result of those actions will be great. You will have more success and enjoyment out of life than ever.

CHAPTER 6: BE IN A CONTINUOUS IMPROVEMENT CYCLE

"I choose to make the rest of my life the best of my life" – Louise Hay

Destined For Greatness

One week prior to writing this chapter, I spoke to a group of 10-15 year-old low-to-middle income kids at the Boys and Girls Club of the Hatchie River Region in Covington, TN. It was at this worldly insignificant place that I had my most significant breakthrough as a person and realized that I truly walked in my purpose for the first time as designed by God. This moment in time was a game changer for me and will forever be emblazoned in my memory as the first group of individuals who received a word from God through me in its purest form.

There are several reasons that made this day and this moment so special and great for me. The Boys and Girls Club of the Hatchie River Region is two blocks down the street from my childhood home and in the same park location where I was teased as a kid but was now mentoring, educating and ministering to the new generation of children who needed a word from God to let them know that they matter, someone else cares, they can escape the small confines of their home town and neighborhood and do great things in the world. How do I know that? I know because I was one of those kids in the same situation 20 to 25 years ago.

My parents, whom I love, adore and respect for everything they have done for me in my life, were the recipients of a miracle from God when they birthed me. Before you start thinking I'm some egotistical, self-centered person, let me tell you why I say I am a miracle from God. I was born in 1979 nearly three months premature. I'm not sure about premature birth statistics in 1979, but let me give you a few recent statistics per the Centers of Disease Control and Prevention:

- Preterm birth is the birth of an infant prior to 37 weeks of pregnancy
- Nearly 500,000 babies are preterm each year (1 in 8 infants born in the United States)
- 35% of infant deaths in 2009 are attributed to preterm birth
- Preterm birth is the leading cause of neurological disabilities in children

Given these recent statistics, one can imagine how difficult it was to survive a premature or preterm birth 35 years ago.

Well, it was indeed much worse. I always think back to the first time my parents told me how fortunate I am to be on this earth, and I carry myself with more confidence on tough days. Why? Doctors gave my parents a very difficult prognosis upon my grand entrance into the world. As a 23-week old infant, I was birthed by emergency C-section in Memphis, TN. Shortly after the elation of seeing my entrance into the world, I was hurried off to the neonatal intensive care unit or NICU. Remember again that it was 1979. There were very few high tech and advanced methods to get a preterm infant the great medical care that we have today.

What drives me every day and gives me even more motivation to do more and be great is the understanding of God's miracles and how I am one of them. Doctors gave my parents some very tough news when I was born. The mental imagery of my father telling me my story for the first time when I was around eight or nine years old sticks with me like a fresh wound. Doctors came to my parents and said, "Well Mr. and Mrs. Young, we hate to inform you, but your son only has a maximum of 30 days to live." As one can imagine, my parents were devastated. My father went on to elaborate at how small I was. My father isn't a large man by any means but average size with rather large hands for his stature. He told me how he could hold me, my entire body, in the palm of his hand. I immediately said "you're joking". Yet, he was not. His memory of my birth was a fresh wound as well because his eyes welled up a little as he was telling me this.

He said, "Marques, I'm not kidding. I could hold your entire body in the palm of my hand. It hurt me so much to have to see you with all of the tubes in you and not be able to take you home like we wanted to." You know how kids think that their parents are invincible and can do anything, and especially a son about his father. I had never seen my dad get so emotional with me, but I was glad. It was at that moment that I realized how special life is, how special my life is, and how special I could be. I was destined for greatness, just as we all are, and I must take advantage of every opportunity that I have in life.

In addition to being a high risk, preterm infant, I was also raised in a low-to-middle income environment in rural West Tennessee. Fortunately for me, I did have a great support system with loving parents, grandparents and family who always believed in

51

me. For the first four to five years of my life, we lived primarily with my grandparents in Mason, TN. Looking back on it, the family situation was one from a movie about a rural farming community and African-American families living in the South. We had multiple generations living in one household on a farm complete with livestock, pigs, chickens, hunting dogs (they were mutts), and a lot of love.

Not to get into my family history, but this situation was another miracle as this family was not my biological family. However, they are family and that's all that matters. When you have people who love you and care about you unconditionally and want to see you be the best person possible, regardless of who they are, they are important in your life and can even be more important and have a greater impact than your parents, siblings or other relatives.

My non-biological grandmother and grandfather lived in the house along with my grandmother's father and her aunt and uncles. I believe in total there were at least eight of us living there at the time. Until my grandmother's recent passing, I was not completely aware of how fortunate and blessed I was to be raised in such humble yet great circumstances. The family owned not only the land where the house stood, but the majority of the land in the community, upwards of more than 250 acres! Yes, I was born into local greatness in a small rural farming community, and the family gave other families land to build homes and raise their families dating back to the 1800s. The entire community was based on the greatness within the household and family in which I was blessed to be a member of through the graces of God.

My grandmother's funeral was full of stories about how she, my grandfather and my family were the backbone of the community. Educators who religiously taught Sunday school at Hopewell Baptist Church and had long-standing, 30+ year careers as teachers at local schools. It seemed as though they took everyone to the malls and shops in Memphis to get school clothes every year and supply the needs of families in need whenever someone needed a little help. I learned that greatness begets greatness, and greatness only takes a little push to keep the momentum going for years and generations to come.

After my grandmother's funeral, I spent time with my father and wife driving around the community learning more about my history that I did not know. During these moments and the days afterwards, I reflected on my life and shared some of those moments with the crowd of 20 or so 10-to-15 year olds at the Boys and Girls Club. It was this moment that I realized that not only was I groomed for greatness, but it is my assignment to groom others for greatness too.

Desire Determines Your Greatness

As I shared my story with the room full of boys, I saw myself in each of them as they sat attentively listening to the words I had to say. After moving from my grandparent's home, we eventually moved into my parent's current home that is just down the street from the Boys and Girls Club. I shared with the boys how I know that I was made to be great, but it required work on my part to create greatness in situations that discouraged and even destroyed greatness for many others that I knew.

As a premature child, I was small during my childhood and teenage years. I was generally the smallest kid in the bunch, but I never acted like it. That's because my parents and grandparents, including my father's parents who lived in Covington next door to us on the adjacent street, always encouraged me and told me that I was smart and special. Now, you must also understand that having two grandparents and a mother as educators gave me very little recourse other than being a very studious child, and I am very thankful for it. As a small kid, I had to make up for the challenges of being the runt, and I did that by being smarter than most and working harder than everyone else at everything I did.

Engineered For Success

Aside from baseball, I loved playing sports and played everything imaginable that was available to me including football, basketball, tennis and swimming. The only sport I didn't play growing up was golf. My mother tried to get me to play on numerous occasions, but I declined thinking it was too unconventional for me as a young kid from "the hood". Looking back, I now realize that I was fearful of what others would say about me. It's actually ironic because she asked me about golf while I was in high school. By this point in my life, I had overcome the teasing of others due to my size, small ears, big teeth, and even being called an Uncle Tom. Yes, I had ignorant kids in the neighborhood who called me terrible names

55

because I was doing more to better myself which required me to venture outside of our predominantly Black neighborhood to do things with my non-Black friends. I was one of the few kids from my neighborhood to venture out, and I did so very routinely. I realized early on that you must broaden your horizons and eliminate negative people from your circles. Negative people will never help you become great and will do nearly anything and everything possible to derail you from reaching your dreams and goals.

Today I cherish those days of being teased. The teasing increased my hunger and desire to be great and get out of that environment. Fortunately, God gave me more and more opportunities to do just that, and I took action and reaped great results. I graduated in the Top 10 of my high school class with honors and eventually went on to graduate from The University of Tennessee with a Bachelor's of Science degree in Mechanical Engineering. Today I am the Maintenance Manager of the largest ice cream manufacturing facility in the United States and soon the world and am responsible for maintaining millions of dollars of assets that employs hundreds of people in my hometown of Covington, TN. Yes, here is another moment of irony. Most of those same kids who teased me

56

for years either currently work for or with me or need me to help them get a job at the facility where I am the only Black member of the Plant Leadership team. I have shot several videos and conducted numerous interviews for the company about our plant and the City of Covington.

Each and every day I have people who come to me and say how proud they are of what I have accomplished or how they can't believe how I was able to get to where I am today. For those who ask how, it is simple. I believed in myself. I had a dream and developed a plan to accomplish that dream. Once the plan was developed, action was taken to accomplish the goals to reach my dreams. I then began to walk in my purpose by mentoring others and sharing my story with them just as I am sharing some of my story in this book with you.

During my working career, I have worked for three Fortune 500 companies and have been a key member of the organization in each of those companies. I have been responsible for managing and maintaining millions of dollars of assets while creating new processes and systems to drive improvement and profits. As an accomplished manager and leader, I am finally reaching my full potential as a leader now that I have learned my purpose and begin to walk in my purpose.

Today I give you a personal challenge and charge – have a one-on-one talk with God. Ask Him to help you identify your purpose and your assignment. No matter what you are doing today, if you are not living in your purpose, you are not maximizing your potential. Challenge yourself to be great each and every day. Your future depends on it.

Maintenance Is Required

After spending the past 12 years in manufacturing facilities within the food and beverage industry, I've learned it is extremely critical to perform maintenance on the assets most important to your operation in order to maximize profits by minimizing waste. The consumer does not want to carry the burden of paying for excess production time, materials or labor due to inefficiencies and ineffectiveness within the manufacturing process. Additionally, equipment and asset maintenance should be routine and proactive versus emergency maintenance. The difference between the two has huge implications on the overall effectiveness and profit of the operation.

Emergency maintenance occurs when equipment unexpectedly breaks down and causes production to stop. In a food environment there are certain guidelines and regulations that must be followed, and when unexpected production stoppages occur, the product manufacturer may be required to discard that product due to the inability to meet those strict guidelines and requirements. Emergency maintenance is unplanned and completely reactive. The maintenance and operations personnel must deal with the current conditions and resources available to make the necessary repairs to return the equipment to an operational state, and sometimes this may not be possible if parts, materials or labor resources are unavailable. More time is required to find parts, materials or labor to return the equipment back to its normal state.

Conversely, routine and proactive maintenance is typically a planned event with controlled shutdowns to provide the optimal conditions to execute the maintenance activities for the asset and ensure it is returned to its prime operating state. The manufacturer has removed all obstacles and has identified what exactly needs to be repaired or addressed within a determined amount of time to return the equipment or asset back to production and maximize output and profits. This routine preventive or proactive maintenance may only require some minor inspections and repairs instead of repairing broken or severely damaged components, or sometimes, a complete overhaul, rebuild or replacement of an asset. Spare parts are kept in inventory to maintain the equipment using planned maintenance activities through a preventive maintenance program.

What does any of this talk of emergency versus routine and preventive maintenance have to do with your greatness? It has everything to do with your greatness. Just like the equipment used for manufacturing, if you are always in an emergency or reactive state, you do not have the time to focus and develop a strategy (DREAM); you do not have time to develop a plan (PLAN); you cannot take action on the things that you desire or need to address in life to fulfill your assignment because you are always working on something besides your purpose (ACTION); you have a difficult time getting out of the vicious cycle because you are like a firefighter running from one fire to the next trying to stay alive.

Those temporary or emergency repairs are like Band-Aids because the root-cause of the issue is never addressed. Band-Aids are adhesive bandages used to protect cuts, scraped knees and boo-

boos that you can often apply to the wound without assistance. The proactive repairs are like routine doctor's examinations. You as the patient receive a more thorough inspection of your height, weight, vital signs and any abnormal symptoms or medical issues. The doctor is preventing you from falling into poor health or, if you are already ill, developing any worse symptoms or conditions. You don't spend too much time there and can leave with a clean bill of health or a prescription to resolve your issue in a certain amount of time. The doctor schedules follow up visits for either your next routine check up or your evaluation of the existing condition to make sure you are getting healthy. You have a definitive understanding of what is next and can plan your future accordingly.

Maintenance is required to continue to walk in your purpose, fulfill your assignment and be great. Like the factory equipment, it is easy to turn on the power and run the machine, but it cannot run forever without some maintenance. Things will get jammed inside the machine, an operator can change how it functions, or it may need to be cleaned. Some form of maintenance is required to sustain its operation. You must continually seek assistance from others to maintain the greatness within you, and primarily seek assistance from

61

God. He will impart His unyielding grace, wisdom and mercy on you during your walk to stay at your peak operating condition. Even when an occasional emergency happens, you will be better prepared to respond because your plan is defined. You have resources to assist you through the emergency without spending time finding a solution. Equipment comes with an owner's manual, and so does your life with the Bible. Use it to eliminate or minimize unexpected breakdowns and keep your well-oiled machine primed at peak operating condition to maximize your throughput and your profits.

CHAPTER 7: AVOID AVERAGE & EMBRACE YOUR GREATNESS

Matthew 22:14 "For many are called, but few are chosen." – The Bible

Average Is A Disease

After graduating from college with a Mechanical Engineering degree, I chose to enter the work force instead of pursuing one of my dreams to become a sports agent. It was a tough decision for me at the time. I was accepted to Ohio State University's Fisher School of Business and had a great offer from a premier Fortune 200 company to quickly move up the career ladder and become virtually anything that I wanted to be...yeah, you know the dream that is sold! Needless to say, I entered the work force with a great job that had amazing salary and benefits for a young 23-year-old from little old Covington, TN.

During the past 12 years, I've had great experiences and moved up the ranks with three well-known global companies. Each experience involved me transforming a facility into a world-class manufacturing site, increasing production output, reducing costs and growing profits as a Maintenance Manager. I have had the responsibility of maintaining the assets and infrastructure of large manufacturing facilities with budgets upwards of $15-20 million dollars under my direct control. I was a "clean up man" in all of my jobs. In every role at every facility that I worked, I had to develop better processes, procedures and systems to improve the operations and maintenance programs to increase profits. Each and every time I succeeded.

It was only a year ago that I realized what God was doing for me during these 12 years with the immense responsibilities, budgets and pressures to manage and lead large teams. He was giving me these experiences in preparation to walk in my purpose and fulfill my assignment. As a child I faced adversity from the day I was born, overcame teasing, became an above average baseball player in my own right, and excelled academically. To date, I have helped thousands, if not millions, of people enjoy products and services through my good works as a skilled and successful Maintenance Manager and leader.

However, I never was fulfilled until I returned home to Tennessee in my current capacity. I am still working as a Maintenance Manager and executing even greater things with my current circumstances. The primary difference is that now I have started a few businesses of my own and am helping individuals become debt free, realize their potential as a gift from God, and groom them for greatness using my journey as evidence that it can and will happen for you. All of those experiences have provided me with documented evidence that He is real, and He will make a way for you to walk in your greatness when the time is right. He provides me everything that I need to have the proper balance to accomplish all of my business requirements and be a great husband and father.

Had I always listened to and adhered to the status quo, I would have been average my entire life. I would have never said "YES" to baseball. I would have never attempted to broaden my horizons and play other sports or meet new people. I would have not been one of the few African-American students at Covington High School to be a National Merit Scholar, receive a fully paid scholarship to attend The University of Tennessee and receive a Mechanical Engineering degree. I would have never been in a position to travel around the country and have companies pay for me to move and relocate. I would have died within 30 days. I would not have written this book that you are reading today that is grooming you for greatness.

Being average is easy. Average is waking up every day and going through the motions. Average is showing up but not giving your maximum effort. Average is making a "C" when you know you can make an "A" with a very little additional effort. Average is working a job that you don't like just because it's easy or you don't want to risk losing what you have for something greater. Average is a disease and an epidemic. God put us here to do great things. To whom much is given, much is required. You were given life. You could have been miscarried, killed in an accident, left for dead. You are here with all of your faculties. Quit being average because it's easy. Get Up, Get Out and Be Great Today!

Greatness Is Risky Business

When I went to the Boys and Girls Club to speak with the youth group, I did not have a speech prepared. I asked God to lead me and direct me based on the environment and the vibe. The only thing that I had prepared was my purpose and two topics – Choices and Fear. God has always placed me in positions to take calculated risks while entrusting both my faith in Him and in me. This time was no different. My 20-minute time allowance turned into a 90-minute outpouring of mentorship to the group. The unadulterated truth about life, the struggles of life, keeping faith in God, believing in yourself, and living by the aforementioned keys and principles in this book is what we talked about as a group. We talked about choices and fear and not allowing others to force you to make bad choices or fear being you because no one else can be you or do what you were put on this earth to do. After that hour and a half, I believe I was more inspired than the kids. This feeling of inspiration and helping others is what counts.

I've been an independent business owner for nearly one full year. The services I provide helps individuals and families become debt free using proven strategies. I spend one-on-one time with individuals and families teaching them financial principles and providing them with proven systems and strategies to minimize their taxes, debt and expenses, create business income, and create generational wealth so that their families can live the lifestyles that they desire. The information that I share with people is straightforward and easy to learn to implement. However, I struggled to build my business as quickly as I desired. People hesitated to walk with me and use these proven systems and strategies that helped me eliminate over $12,000 in debt twice within one year without using loans or getting into some other financial struggle. God blessed me enough with everything he had given me up to that point in time to prevent me from losing my mind with everything that was going with me both personally and professionally. We will save that for perhaps another book at another time.

What I soon learned shocked me. Although I spent time teaching and coaching others with some good results, I did not see my business and my profits elevate until I started walking in my purpose. Speaking with groups or individuals about their lives and sharing my story with them resonated more than me talking with them about their financial goals and dreams and the solutions that I have available for them. People gravitated to my story and learning about my journey. As I helped them see how God has brought me through and given me more and more breakthroughs, I have been able to close more business and help more people start their personal journey to eliminate debt and find their purpose.

Shortly after giving this free service to the community, my business has blown up. That's right...I quickly became a certified author and a publishing company owner. I still have my initial business as a financial coach. I am now a personal development coach and mentor. All of this while still serving in my Maintenance Manager capacity and being a great husband and father for my family. I continue to entrust myself to the Lord and listen to His word. I follow the 7 principles to walk in my purpose, create multiple streams of income and enjoy endless profits.

1. HAVE A DREAM...NOW CHASE IT!

2. PLAN YOUR WORK & WORK YOUR PLAN

3. TAKE IMMEDIATE ACTION

4. TIME IS OF THE ESSENCE...USE YOUR TIME WISELY

5. MAINTAIN YOUR FAITH & FOLLOW YOUR INTUITION

6. BE IN A CONTINUOUS IMPROVEMENT CYCLE

7. AVOID AVERAGE & EMBRACE YOUR GREATNESS

I now have upwards of seven new streams of income that have helped me and my family alleviate our financial burdens because we are now 100% debt free with investment accounts doing the heavy lifting for us. Walking in my purpose has allowed me to create new products and services to help others reach their maximum potential. The amazing part of it all is that it has come easy to me. That's what happens when you walk in your purpose and help others.

God did the heavy lifting when he created you. You just have to listen to Him, stay close to Him, seek guidance from Him and follow the instructions. Regardless of your current wage earning status, business venture, or personal situation, following God's instructions and the 7 Principles will make you emotionally, spiritually and financially wealthy beyond you wildest dreams. I encourage you to step outside of your comfort zone and take action on those things that you've desired to do for so long. Take my journey and continue to groom yourself and others for greatness as you walk in your purpose.

CONCLUSION

Life presents each of us with our own sets of challenges, obstacles and setbacks. No one is exempt from them. The difference between those who are average and those who are great is how one responds to adversity. You will never have that road to Easy Street paved perfectly for you. Even when you get to Easy Street, you must still construct your house because it is not built for you already. No one has the blueprint developed and the house constructed that you desire but you. You must take the necessary steps to build that house and build your future. Your future is destined to be great, but only if you follow the seven principles to discover how to walk in your purpose.

Once you begin to walk in your purpose, you will begin to earn the desires of your heart. You are destined for greatness. Start grooming yourself for greatness. Wake up each and every day with one mission in mind – do what God has put me here to do. If you have not identified what your purpose is yet, do not worry. He will show you, but you MUST constantly talk with God and ask Him to fulfill the desires of your heart. Greatness is in you. Expect nothing less. I thank you for taking the time to read and share this book.

Following the seven principles will yield immediate positive results.

Get Up. Get Out. Be Great Today!

www.ingramcontent.com/pod-product-compliance
Lightning Source LLC
Chambersburg PA
CBHW070116070426
42448CB00040B/3043